D1115471

We Are Human Angels

The 7 keys to overcome the ego
The 7 keys to live with the heart
in service to the Oneness

When we live in the ego, we are human
When we live in the Awareness
of the Oneness,
we are Human Angels

ISBN-13: 978-1492200239
ISBN-10: 1492200239

Original title "Essere Angeli Umani"
Translated from the italian
Translator: Ross Wilkins
mailto: *wilkins.ross@rocketmail.com*
Cover design by Roberto De Gregorio
mailto: *degraf@tin.it*

For more information on all Human Angels' books and the stores where they are available, visit the official site: *www.wearehumanangels.com.*

Thanks, thanks immensely
to all the companions of this journey
To those who have arrived
To those who remained
To those who have fallen away
(But not from the heart)

Human Angels

Foreword

It is a Blessing to me to have been asked to write the Foreword to the Book *"We Are Human Angels"*. As a Licensed Therapist, I would recommend it be given out at all the maternity wards, be a Blessing to others by giving it as a gift, placed in every Christmas Stocking and given as the Afikomen Gift with chocolates. You may ask why? Yet, as I say to many of my clients who look to me for answers, validation and The Truth, "The Heart and Soul Always Knows the Truth".

After reading the last page of *"We Are Human Angels"*, you will have a Divine Moment of Stillness to reflect on all that you read. In that Divine Stillness many of you will feel an Inner Peace for the first time; an Inner Peace you have searched for all of your life. Part of that Inner Peace will be because "Your Heart and Soul" will know it read The Truth; a Truth you know you were Born with. "You Are A Human Angel." And, unlike history that continues to repeat itself, you will know that you no longer need to repeat the patterns in your life that has made you feel stuck, loss, hurt, deprived, alone, short - changed or bear the heavy burdens you have endured.

As you will learn in the Book, "*We Are Human Angels*", living an Ego Driven life created many of these tearful experiences. An Ego Driven life you may have been taught to live by your education, your social circle, your profession and your family patterns through intergenerational transmission.

The Book *"We Are Human Angels"* is the Handbook to now, finally, give you permission to be the True You. You are Divine. You are part of the Oneness. And, your Heart and Soul knows that is the Truth. Your Heart and Soul knows that Love is the Greatest Power in the Universe. Through your life you have seen its Power on one of your tough days and a stranger smiles at you or on a day of sorrow others give you kindness that gives you the Divine energy to continue with your journey. As Human Angels, we let go of the Ego and become that stranger that gives that smile and "the others" who give kindness that gives someone the Divine energy to continue their journey.

Love is Unconditional. Respect is Unconditional. It is Trust that is earned. I write this for those who are at the beginning of their revelation and journey that "They are a Human Angel".

The Book *"We Are Human Angels"* tries to emphasize this by stating that although we are in service to the Oneness, everyone has Free Will. As Human Angels we do not impose on others' Free Will, no matter how much you feel they need it. That is not part of your or their Divine Plan. And, if you insist, most likely chaos will ensure.

I write this information because the book, *"We Are Human Angels"*, is so important to the World and I don't want it to be misunderstood as "Rosy- Colored Literature" full of pretty prose. With the Book, *"We Are Human Angels"* many will awaken and be enlightened to what the heart and soul knows to be the Truth.

Sometimes, you will be a Seed Planter. Sometimes, you will be the Messenger. But, you need to shed the Ego and be reassured that sometimes you need to be the Stillness and only be the witness. As we have entered a new age of Technology that many may have never believed they would have seen in their lifetime, we are also entering an Era of the beginning of many becoming enlightened to the Divine

Oneness Consciousness. And, Your Heart and Soul Knows that to be The Truth because never before in Human History has so many been so educated and never in Human History have we had so many resources available that just needs Divine Wisdom with no Ego to benefit Humankind, because, Love is the Greatest Power in the Universe.

Cherie Mosher, LCSW-R
Author of "Long Island Gold"
and Licensed Therapist

Introduction

Are you a Human Angel?

If since childhood you have wanted to change the world and have not stopped believing...

If you have always dreamed of relieving the sorrows of all living beings...

If you feel that you have a special talent to help others...

If you have an out of the ordinary sensitivity...

If you have overcome difficult trials in your life...

If you think that despite everything, life should be lived with joy...

If, while always trying to give meaning to your suffering, you believe that there must be a way to stop yours and others suffering...

If in your heart there is no room for hatred and resentment...

If you always try to change evil into good and darkness into light...

If you always follow your heart even when it seems to be the hardest thing to do...

If you have always had a vision of heaven on earth and would like to spread it throughout the world...

If you have the ability to read people and know what is hidden within their hearts...

If you silently bless everyone you encounter in your life...

If you, from the very beginning, have always felt a sense of not belonging to this world...

If you have never been able to relate yourself with any group of people, but you have always had a deep desire to connect yourself with your Souls' family here on earth...

If the search for truth is your greatest passion...

If you live with honesty even when it hurts...

If you believe in the healing power of Love...

If you still have the same dreams you had when you were a pure-hearted child...

If you feel you were born for a greater purpose and would like to express it...

...you are a Human Angel and you are just trying to remember.

Human Angels are souls who have chosen to be born now on this planet to awaken themselves and humanity to Unconditional Love and Awareness of the Oneness.

Human Angels are beacons that simply being who they are, illuminate the darkness, to help those who are still on the path to stay the course.

If you feel you are a Human Angel and the time has come to open your heart and unfold your wings, this book is for you. "The 7 Keys to overcome the ego" and "The 7 keys to live with the heart in service to the Oneness" are the titles of the two parts of this book. To guide you, step by step, in your journey from overcoming the ego and suffering, until the fulfillment of your True Nature as a Human Angel.

Part 1
The 7 keys
to overcome the ego

1.1

The Oneness and the ego

How to overcome the ego with the knowledge of the Oneness

The Oneness is complete Life, undivided and indivisible, always present. All Life, despite having many shapes and forms, is One.

The ego is the illusion of separation that makes us believe that there is a distinction between inside and outside, between us and others. The ego is a framework of habits, fears, judgments and prejudices that we call personality or character and that imprisons the accomplishment of our True Nature.

When, looking at our lives, we become aware that we are all One, we realize that there is no separation between us and the world, and that the people we have met in our lives are merely our own projections, as we are theirs, and to a greater or lesser extent, each reflects a part of us: our light and our shadow.

When you judge someone, you are judging yourself. When you hate someone, you are hating yourself. When you love someone, you are loving yourself. (This is the most important of the keys to the Oneness). Nobody will ever betray, humiliate or hurt you, if you have not first betrayed, humiliated or hurt yourself.

Our thoughts, our emotions are powerful and infallible energy fields that attract complementary energies. This is how we co-create every moment in our lives.

Other people, in the role of our mirrors, are neither good nor bad, neither right nor wrong, they are beyond all judgment and simply reflect what we project onto them.

Also the pain that is caused by our mirrors is a gift to be accepted with gratitude, a gift of Love that gives us the opportunity to observe and experience our emotional wounds and to transcend them.

If we learn to observe others as our mirrors to understand who we are, we become deeply aware of our scars and the limiting beliefs through which we co-create our lives.

If, for example, our scars come from issues of abandonment, we co-create, through the limiting belief that "all those who love me will, sooner or later, leave me", then we continue to attract people and situations that will make us experience abandonment, until the time we are no longer afraid of it.

In the Oneness there are neither victims nor persecutors, only bonds of Love entered into by souls before incarnating. In Love for Love's sake.

"In the next life, I will make you suffer, I will be the mirror of your fears, but I will also be the instrument of your awakening. Remember that when the time comes: the faster you remember our covenant of Love, the less suffering you will experience".

And when the reflections that, as mirrors, we emanate, are cleared of every fear and every limiting belief, we finally become whole and pure mirrors of light.

The first key to overcome the ego

Use the reflections of what you see to observe and recognize yourself. We are all One and others are simply reflections of ourselves. When the mirror is cleared, the reflection becomes clean too.

1.2

Judgment
How to overcome the matrix of the ego

When we recognize ourselves as an indivisible part of the Oneness, we experience joy. When, however, identifying with the ego, we separate ourselves from the Oneness, we experience duality and suffering.

Overcoming the ego is removing the root cause. Feelings of pain, worry, shame, or a sense of guilt (the infinite ego symptoms) are a consequence of a single matrix: the illusion of duality that is judgment.

Our thoughts themselves bring judgment and duality: each concept is understood by our mind only when compared to their opposite. The meaning of "health", for example, can be understood only if compared to that of "disease". The meaning of "justice" can only be understood when compared to that of "injustice."

In the Oneness, everything simply Is. Light is not the opposite of dark: Light simply Is. Love is not the opposite of hate: Love simply Is. Life is not the opposite of death:

Life simply Is. Unity is not the opposite of duality: Unity simply Is.

We cannot embrace the Oneness, the Absolute, through the mind. We only have a relative understanding: everything we can know through the mind is only the illusion of separation.

The Oneness cannot be separated into mental categories, because this necessarily involves duality and judgment: we can only experience it and demonstrate it through the evidence of our behaviour.

When we judge ourselves and others, we forget that we are an indivisible part of the Oneness and so we suffer continuously because of the illusion of separation.

When judgment separates us from the Oneness, only total and unconditional acceptance (of ourselves and others) can re-unite us with the Oneness, becoming part of the flow of Life and the Uni-versal plan of Love.

Without judgment, the ego dies and takes with it all the burden of suffering that weighs on our lives. And we begin to unconditionally love ourselves and others.

Only when we stop judging can we truly love. When our quiet mind silences all judgment, can we finally rest in the infinite bliss of the Oneness.

The second key to overcome the ego

Ego is based on judgment. Stop judging and you will be free from the ego: in the Oneness there is no judgment, only Unconditional Love.

1.3

Feelings of guilt
How to stop self-destructive feelings

We are responsible for everything that happens in our lives: responsible but not guilty.

A sense of guilt is one of the most powerful traps used by the ego to keep us glued to the old, to fear and to suffering. A sense of guilt arises when we judge ourselves and others: it is the direct and inevitable consequence of judgment;

We are the most implacable judges of ourselves, we judge continuously and, in addition, we project onto ourselves what we believe to be the opinions of others. Judgment always brings with it a sense of guilt.

Adam and Eve (*) felt separated from God as a result of having eaten the fruit from the Tree of the Knowledge of Good and Evil (judgment) and because of this they judged God, they judged themselves and therefore, felt guilty. So they began to experience fear and pain.

Similarly, when, like Adam and Eve, we give power to duality and ego, through judging, we separate ourselves from the Oneness, we leave the Paradise of our Universal soul (the Higher Self) and our lives become a hell of guilt and unfulfilled atonement.

Therefore, a sense of guilt is the most powerful obstacle to the accomplishment of ourselves: we become our own worst enemies. Our attempts at fulfillment will fail due to our own destructive feelings of guilt and therefore we do not feel worthy or adequate.

When we are happy, we feel guilty as if our happiness is an insult to those who suffer. When we receive love and attention, we feel guilty and uncomfortable, because we feel we are not worthy of it.

When we allow ourselves to be ourselves, we feel guilty, because in this way we disappoint those who (parents, children, partners, friends,...), would like us to be different, each according to their own expectations projected onto us.

But if there is no judgment, there is neither fault nor sin, so the ego disappears and everything returns to belong to the Oneness. And we finally have the courage to be ourselves, to be accomplished and happy.

The third key to overcome the ego

It takes more courage to be yourself than to live in the prison of ego with feelings of guilt. It takes a lot more courage to be happy than to be unhappy.

(*) From the Christian Bible and Torah. Genesis, 2.16-17 and 3.6; Adam and Eve's disobedience to God is also mentioned in the Quran.

1.4

Projections
How to heal our romantic relationships

Romantic relationships are a major cause of suffering. Each of us experiences, through relationships, the highest joys but also the deepest sufferings: betrayal, abandonment, resentment, anger, disappointed expectations, a sense of failure...

But, in relationships, when there is suffering there cannot be true love: true Love is Unconditional. Either Love is joy and happiness, or it is not Unconditional Love.

When there is suffering, it is the "love of the ego". What we feel in our romantic relationships, that we believe is love, is actually a tangled web of projective mechanisms of the ego: "I project my father onto you and you project your mother onto me."

The partner is no longer seen for whom she or he is, but through the distorting mirror of parental relationships that we have internalized and that we continue to project onto them. The stronger the projection mechanism, the stronger the feelings of pain in the relationship become.

We can also change our partner, but, in reality, if we do not heal and cleanse our projective mechanisms, our partner will recite the same role, continuing to act as a mirror of our deepest scars.

For example, as a boy, if I had a controlling and "emasculating" mother, my partner will always behave with me in a similar fashion, until I heal the feminine side that I have internalized.

Only looking at myself without judgment, can I accept myself for who I am and let go of the illusion of control and "emasculation" that I have co-created in my life.

For example, as a girl, if I had a father who had behaved in a disparaging and denigrating way towards my mother, my partner will do the same with me, until I heal my sense of self-worthlessness.

Judging your partner, thinking of them as being wrong, is but a trick of the ego: "They are immature" or "selfish", or "not reliable" or "unfaithful" or "afraid of my love", "...".

If you judge your partner from outside the perspective of the Oneness, separate from yourself, how can you really love them? Use your partner as a mirror to see yourself more intimately and deeply and start to feel that you are your partner and your partner is you, beyond any judgment. Begin to recognize and to accept yourself through them.

The recognition of love that is denied by your partner is the recognition of love that you are denying yourself.

Healing our wounds, we rebalance in order to achieve the Sacred Union of our inner feminine and masculine sides, rejoining ourselves in Love with Love.

And, after clearing our mirrors of any projecting mechanisms, having harmonized and integrated the duality of the feminine and masculine sides within ourselves, we can achieve the Sacred Union through Unconditional Love, in the joy of giving and receiving freely.

The Sacred Union is our accomplishment: finally, we realize that everything we are looking for we have already found within ourselves and that now we only have to fully express it in our lives.

The fourth Key to overcome the ego

Your partner is your deepest mirror: do not expect them to change. Healing yourself, you heal your relationship. Healing yourself, you achieve the Sacred Union.

1.5

Forgiveness
How to free ourselves from the suffering of the past

The past continues to live within us and, although we try to rid ourselves of it, the old suffering continues to echo within us and produce new distress.

Only forgiveness can free us from the past and undo the old ties, opening our hearts to a paradise of gratitude. But to do this, we must first cleanse our cellular memory from the anger and resentment that the illusion of separation has imprinted onto our cells.

To forgive others, in order to forgive ourselves, because in their roles as our mirrors, they have been nothing other than a tool to our lack of self-love, a lack of self-recognition, and a lack of self-respect.

Only through forgiving can we understand that there is nothing and no one to forgive. And that we too, if we have hurt someone, have been for them, nothing more than an instrument of Love in the same way they have been for us. In the Oneness there is no separation, no judgment, and everything happens in Divine Perfection.

Forgiveness that comes from the ego is an act of true presumption: "Even if you were wrong, I am so good and magnanimous to forgive you."

From the perspective of the Oneness, we forgive by becoming aware that we are the co-creators of our own suffering: "I forgive you. You have been my mirror through which I could understand how much I did not love myself. I feel for you the most profound gratitude. Thanks to you I have become conscious of my wounds and am now able to observe, recognize and heal them." In doing this, we do not necessarily need to interact with the other person, we can talk to them at soul level.

Anger and resentment, however, keep us anchored to the past and perpetuate the link with all those who have made us suffer or that we caused to suffer.

There can be no true overcoming of the ego without forgiveness in the Oneness. "Now I can let you go, I forgive you and I forgive myself. I bless you and thank you. Now that I have freed you, I too am free."

Forgiveness frees the forgiver. The act of

forgiveness unties each and every knot. Only Love and gratitude can set us free.

The fifth key to overcome the ego

When you forgive others, in order to forgive yourself, you become free from the past and are able to understand that there is really nothing and no one to forgive. In the Oneness everything happens because of Love.

1.6

Fear
How to overcome the illusion of fear

When we become aware that the only reality is Oneness and that we are that Oneness, our hearts fill with joy and every fiber of our being is full of Love. And it is then that the darkness (even the deepest part of it) that still lurks within us is illuminated by the intense light that we embody: everything that separates us from the Oneness manifests in order to be recognized and released.

We face our fears in order to overcome the ego and the illusion of separation and to be reborn to Love in Unity. We do not have to take any action because it is our own fears that call into our lives those events and those people that let us learn from our experiences in order to free ourselves of those fears.

Therefore, every trial in our life is a gift, an opportunity that we ourselves have chosen, so that we can dispel the darkness that we bring in and make room for the light. Only riding the tiger can we realize that it is not real and that it is only a paper tiger.

In fact, when we finally look at ourselves with courage through the mirror of our fears, we discover that what we feared only existed in our minds: fear is the memory of pain (the past) and the attempt to avoid it (the future). Fear is always separation from the present.

Fear is also moving away from our True Selves, that is from the Oneness: when we feel separated from the Whole, we believe that there is something or someone outside of us to be afraid of.

When we feel fear, we deny our True Nature, forgetting that, as an indivisible part of the Oneness, we have the same creative power as the Oneness. As we have unconsciously created our fears, similarly, we can consciously decree their end and start to create only what we choose to create.

We experience who we aren't in order to remember who we Are and to express our Divine Nature.

When we are prey to our fears, we have to remember that we are giving power to that which does not exist. And remember that the only reality is Unconditional Love: the eternal, immutable state of Being.

Fear enslaves us, Truth sets us free and the only Truth is the Oneness.

Experiencing fear and overcoming it, opens our hearts to Compassion: any fear and pain, once transmuted into Awareness and Love, becomes a precious flower to share with others in Unity.

The sixth key to overcome the ego

When you feel fear, you are experiencing the ego and the illusion of separation. When you feel Unconditional Love, you are experiencing your Divine Nature in the Oneness.

1.7

Acceptance
*How to make the final transition
from the ego to the Oneness*

The practice of Unconditional Love starts with the full acceptance of ourselves, just as we are: self acceptance does not mean that we stop trying to improve ourselves, it does mean that we start to value and unconditionally love ourselves.

The total acceptance of ourselves in the present moment without judging things that happen, letting things happen as they happen, is the final act that frees us from the ego: this is the unconditional surrender of the ego to the Higher Self.

When we recognize our Divine Nature and we choose to manifest it, we cease to identify with the ego and we rely on our Higher Self, the Uni-versal soul that is the cause and purpose of our lives, the bridge that unites opposites, reconnecting us to the Oneness and to Unconditional Love, beyond any separation.

Judgment, attachments to our past, the fear of loss, fear of change lead us to attempt to control our lives and crystallize in forms that, sooner or later, produce suffering. The ego cannot live in the present, the Here and Now, because it continually produces projections and fantasies, having the illusion of directing the flow of life.

But planning or not, life goes on anyway, whether we try to control events or not, things happen in any case.

True acceptance has nothing to do with passivity: true acceptance means that we stop re-acting through the ego, hurting others and ourselves, and that we start acting with Compassion and the power of Love. Acceptance always leads us to the wisest choices.

When we begin to accept things as they are without judging them, we realize that everything that happens is Divine Perfection and that life is always a blessing.

Yes! We simply have to say an unconditional yes to life and everything follows. The future comes naturally to us without us trying to anticipate it with our fears and projections.

We lose in order to find. We forget in order to remember. We die a death in the ego in order to be reborn in the Oneness, until the end of all our duality, until we become

Human Angels: aware, compassionate messengers of Love in service to the Oneness.

Only when the mind is in a state of stillness can the ego surrender and our hearts can finally make their voices heard in order to be reconnected with our True Self and with all the wisdom of the Uni-verse that has always been within us.

Our Higher Self is the master of Love, in our Higher Self we stop self-judging and learn to accept and love ourselves for who we are, beyond any judgment. We also learn to accept and love others for who they are: loving ourselves in the Unity, we love life in its entirety.

When we try to control our lives through the ego, we are human and we express only what we think is in our possibilities. We create within the limits that we think we have.

When we surrender completely to our Higher Self and we remember that we are Divine Beings, that we are Human Angels, the illusion of having limits vanishes and everything, including miracles, becomes possible in the name of Love.

The seventh key to overcome the ego

When the mind is silent, you can listen to your heart and remember that everything is Love and that you are that Love.

Part 2
The 7 keys
to live with the heart
in service to the Oneness

2.1

The Rebirth
How to be a Human Angel

When the ego and all its illusions die, we are reborn into the Oneness and we can finally express what we really are: Human Angels, souls who have incarnated in order to awaken themselves and others to the Awareness of the Oneness.

By witnessing who we are, we emit light and our light arrives, naturally and spontaneously, where it is needed, where there still lurks the illusion of darkness. Like beacons, we illuminate the route of those who are still traveling through the treacherous waters of the ego: this is the role we have chosen for ourselves as Human Angels.

We do not therefore need to say, to explain or try to convince, but simply by being who we Are, we remind others of their own Divine Nature. We become mirrors for those who, choosing to die in the ego, want to reflect in us in order to be reborn into the Oneness.

When we recognize our Divine Nature, we also begin to see that Divinity is everywhere and we realize that we do not need specific times or sacred places in which to meditate or pray: in the Oneness, everything is Divine, every moment is meditation and prayer and every place is sacred.

In the Oneness, nobody, including Human Angels, is special. In the Oneness everything is Love, and everyone, (whatever they do and beyond any judgment) is, consciously or unconsciously, but still indivisibly, part of the Uni-versal project of Love.

Life becomes our supreme master, we honor and bless Life, recognizing that, by dealing with our most difficult trials, we have reached the highest point of awareness.

This does not mean that suffering is the only way to overcome the ego, but very often it is the path that our souls have chosen to deeply experience duality.

It is not by abstaining, but through fully immersing ourselves in the flow of life that we can experience duality in order to transcend all separation, merging into the Oneness: the infinite ocean of pure Bliss,

from which our Higher Self never left. And what we have experienced so far has simply been our journey through the illusion created by the ego.

When we re-unite in the Oneness, suffering fades and even the memory of all the suffering vanishes. The death of the ego finally allows us to be reborn in Love, and this instantly heals all our wounds, cleansing the memory.

Everything we experience is Love and Joy, and everything we remember is our Divine Nature.

The first key to live with the heart in service to the Oneness

When your ego surrenders to the Higher Self, you become a Human Angel: a radiating center of Light, an active and conscious part of the Universal project of Love.

2.2

The Intelligence of the Heart
How to consciously create our own reality

When we live in the ego, we look with our eyes and we listen with our ears. When we are in the Oneness we see, hear, live with the Intelligence of the Heart that is the union of Awareness and Love: our brain and our heart communicate and cooperate in order to consciously create our own reality.

The Intelligence of the Heart spontaneously blooms as soon as we emerge from the separation between the rational and the intuitive, the mental and the emotional, the male and the female sides of our cerebral hemispheres.

When we recognize our Divine Nature in the Oneness, we begin to consciously use the frontal lobe of our brain, beyond the separation of the two hemispheres, which are always related to duality and judgment.

The frontal lobe is also known as the Throne of God, because this is where we create our reality through images that become our life matrix. The frontal lobe forms and hosts those images that are projected onto the mirror of our lives. What happens to us is nothing but a reflection of our mind, which emanates from the frontal lobe.

When we open our hearts to our Higher Self, we begin to create with Awareness and Love and our lives start to flow free and unhindered: we do not have to do anything, everything just happens.

By changing the mirror, the reflection also changes: the reality (romantic relationships, friendships, job, financial security) that we created from duality and ego begins to collapse, because we cease to produce those images that have allowed and sustained their creation.

In reality, what collapses, is only the illusion of what we believed ourselves to be. To finally give way to what we truly Are and to the fulfillment of our new lives.

The Intelligence of the Heart is a Conscious Creation: by manifesting the God within us we begin to create only what we choose to create, no longer through the ego and judgment, but through Love and not for ourselves but for Unity.

So, free from the emotional quagmire of the ego, we become a conscious presence, listening deeply and in deep contact with ourselves and others. It is through the Intelligence of the Heart, that we, Human Angels, become Love in action.

> *The second key to live with the heart in service to the Oneness*
>
> The power to create is inherent in your Divine Nature. When you create with Awareness and Love you manifest who you really Are.

2.3

Integrity
How to be yourself without judgment

Prior to being One with others, we become One with ourselves. A union of emotions, thoughts and actions: in a word, Integrity.

We live with Integrity when there is no separation between our feelings and our actions, our thoughts and our words. We live with Integrity when we do what we feel and say what we think.

We always require courage to express our Integrity without judgment. If there is no integrity, the Self cannot manifest. When there is no Integrity, there is ego and therefore suffering.

All that is founded on Integrity belongs to a wider perspective: that of Oneness. Integrity creates union: of us with ourselves, of ourselves with others.

The new paradigm of relations is founded on Integrity: Integrity is the pure interaction cleared of any projection, expectation, manipulation or control.

When we live with Integrity every word, thought and action springs from the

Intelligence of the Heart and flows in harmony, enlightened by the pure light of Consciousness.

When we live with Integrity, our intentions are always clear, pure and direct. When instead we act without integrity, our intentions are concealed, most of the time even to ourselves, due to lack of awareness; so that, whatever the nature of our purpose, be it material or immaterial, will be achieved through manipulation and control.

Living without Integrity: "I behave this way, because I think that in this way I will achieve my goal."

Living with Integrity: "I show my purpose with honesty, because as results and goals are not important to me, I do not expect anything at all, I only want to show who I am: I'm my own purpose."

Through Integrity all shadows disappear and we become diamonds: every facet of our being (emotions, feelings, thoughts, actions...), cleansed from the stains of ego, emanates the same pure light.

The third key to live with the heart in service to the Oneness

Only by living with Integrity, can you witness the Oneness. Living with Integrity you can fully express your purpose and all the purity of your Being.

2.4

The Here and Now

How to live free from the past and the future

Time is an illusion, the past and the future are illusions too. In Being nothing really happens, because the Being is the truth behind the happening: the occurrence is the illusion that hides the Being.

The past and the future exist only if we think about them. Linear time (the division of time into the past, present and future) belongs to the ego. When we live in a linear fashion, the future becomes the inevitable consequence of our past.

In linear time, we project onto our future the images and the shadows of our past: this is why we continue to create solely on the basis of patterns of thoughts and behavior which have been tried and tested many times, repeating the same experiences, without considering how these experiences have already caused us to suffer.

The past and the future are tools of the ego that render us finite. Without our judgments about the past (memories) and without our judgments about the future (expectations), there is only the Here and Now, the eternal present, the timeless time of the Oneness.

When we live fully in the Here and Now, every fear, concern and pain vanishes and we are finally free to be who we Are and to manifest our Divine Nature. Yesterday I was, tomorrow I will be, but only Here and Now I Am.

The Here and Now relieves us from the shackles of the past and so that we can regain all the energy wasted in supporting our old creations. In the Here and Now every moment contains an unlimited universe of possibilities that become instantly available to our conscious creation.

The Here and Now is the time of the Human Angels, the time in which the impossible becomes possible. The impossible simply happens when we cease to believe the illusion of having limits.

In the Here and Now, through ourselves, the Being becomes Present, becomes a Presence.

The fourth key to live with the heart in service to the Oneness

Live in the Here and Now without memories (the past) and expectations (the future). Live in the Here and Now and you will be reborn into Love at every moment.

2.5

Free Will
How to help others while respecting their choices

To feel deeply the suffering of others and to know how to help them is a gift that we, as Human Angels, possess. How much pain do we see around us? And how strong is our desire to help others whenever and however?

But helping someone at all costs, means violating the Sacred Law of Free Will. When someone is suffering, we can offer, always and anyway, to be there for them, but we are free to intervene only when we have the consent of their soul.

"Remember: darkness is an illusion that disappears with the light.

When you decide, I'll be there for you, but the decision must be yours."

Souls, before incarnating choose, with Free Will, which path to journey down: what steps to take, which trials to face for their evolution.

And if they still do not learn from the trials of the past, they will continue to face similar trials until they consciously decide to turn their experiences into Awareness and Love.

Nobody can do this for themselves, not even a Human Angel. If we want to help someone at any cost, we interfere with the journey of their soul, replacing their free choice to decide, how and when, they recognize their own divinity, and thus we expose ourselves, in our turn, to pain and frustration.

Every human being, as God incarnate in a body, is the only and absolute creator of their own existence. By recognizing and honoring God in others, we recognize and honor God within ourselves.

According to the Sacred Law of Free Will, we can only wait until others, if and when, are ready to ask for our help, whether through words or silently, it doesn't matter: we feel their request for help coming from their hearts to ours. Only then can we intervene and bear witness to Love.

In the meantime, as Human Angels, with our hearts full of compassion, we will honor those courageous souls that have chosen such turbulent paths to awaken and ascend to the light, to return to where they have always been, in perpetuity, in the bliss of the Oneness.

The fifth key to live with the heart in service to the Oneness

Help others while respecting the Sacred Law of Free Will. By recognizing and honoring God in others, you recognize and honor God within yourself.

2.6

Silence
How a Human Angel prays

How do Human Angels pray? If once prayer was a dialogue or request to a God outside of ourselves, now that we are aware of our Divine Nature what is the point of praying? Simply by remaining silent to hear our Higher Selves, we connect with the Divine within ourselves.

The ego constantly produces thoughts, and as a consequence of these thoughts, everything happens in the mirror of our minds as a reflection of our thoughts. They appear and disappear in our minds and we can observe them and let them go without judging, without judging ourselves. We can simply remain silent, be attentive and present, but not involved.

Thinking belongs to duality. Love belongs to the Oneness. There is no thought without judgment, there is no Unconditional Love without the silence of the mind.

When we become Human Angels, the mind stills so that the heart can speak. We stop paying attention to our thoughts and begin to devote ourselves to the silent spaces between one thought and another, with the purpose of progressively prolonging their lifetimes.

As a consequence of this, the idea of asking, praying and being focused, lose their meaning because the act of asking through the mind is an act of the ego, limiting our Higher Self. By overcoming the ego we leave our Higher Self free to manifest itself in the Unity.

When we do not create joy and abundance, even when we wish for it, this means that our ego is still obstructing what we wish for, continuing to project, onto our lives, images that we created through judgment and limiting beliefs.

It is therefore not by asking, praying, or being focused that we can manifest ourselves. By relying on the silence of the mind, leaving our Higher Self free to create and manifest in the Unity, we finally open our lives to the experience of Love, Joy and Abundance that is the birthright of every human being.

"When you recognize your True Nature, you are God. Thy will be done in the Oneness."

The sixth key to live with the heart in service to the Oneness

In the Oneness, prayer is the stillness of the mind. Reset your thoughts and your Higher Self will be free to create your new reality. Clear your mind and you will be filled by the Love of the Oneness.

2.7

The Greater Good
How to live in service to the Oneness

When we remember that we are Human Angels, we recognize ourselves in the Oneness and we clear the separation between us and everyone else, between us and the entire Uni-verse.

In the Oneness we are everything without judgment: we are the sun, we are the cloud, we are the ocean, we are the wind, we are the storm, we are saints, we are sinners, we are the enemy, we are friends. We are the question, we are the answer: We Are.

And so we come naturally to understand that we no longer have personal goals to achieve and that the only important goal is the Greater Good: the Good that includes and transcends the lives of everyone.

When we remember who we Are, Awareness and Love join together with our Will to create and manifest in the Oneness.

This does not mean that we cease to wish for health, pleasure, or happiness for ourselves; rather, it means that we begin working to ensure that what we manifest for ourselves is part of the divine plan of the Oneness.

Outside of the Oneness, there cannot be true fulfillment and our energies will always be limited. However, when we merge with the Oneness, we become the Oneness, we align and synchronize with the creative matrix of the All and our energies become unlimited. Only the energy of the Oneness is infinite and omnipotent because this is the energy of Life itself.

In becoming One with Life, everyone can draw from the same source of energy: the higher our intentions rise the greater will be the energy that the Universe makes available to us to satisfy them.

When we recognize that our personal good coincides with the Good of everyone, our inner light is turned on: at this point, when a human being becomes a Human Angel, their light, like a beacon, shines all around.

The more lights are lit, the more humanity will be enlightened in these dark times, when the world of the ego, driven to its extreme, has begun its dramatic collapse.

In the meantime we, living with the heart in service to the Oneness, creating with Awareness and Love, living with Integrity, helping others in respect to the Sacred Law of Free Will, relying on our Higher Selves, simply by being who we are, Human Angels, we radiate Light, a Light that in these dark times is truly needed by humanity.

The seventh key to live with the heart in service to the Oneness

Live with your heart in service to the Oneness: Oneness is the Key and Unity is the way.

Appendix

Being Human Angels

- ❖ When we live in the ego, we are human. When we live in the Awareness of the Oneness, we are Human Angels.
- ❖ When we love without judgment, unconditionally, we are Human Angels.
- ❖ When, as midwives, we help others to be reborn into the Oneness, we are Human Angels.
- ❖ When we create with Awareness and Love, we are Human Angels.
- ❖ When, in the silence of our minds we listen to the voices of our hearts, we are Human Angels.
- ❖ When we are Love in action, ready to help and support others in respect to the Free Will of every soul, we are Human Angels.
- ❖ When we live our lives with Integrity for ourselves and for our relationships, we are Human Angels.
- ❖ When, through us, the Oneness becomes Present, becomes a Presence, we are Human Angels.

- ❖ When we testify to the truth of the Oneness, giving ourselves in the service of the Greater Good, we are Human Angels.
- ❖ When at last we remember who we Are, then we are Human Angels.

About the authors

You will not find our names as we have chosen to pen this book as Human Angels, a collective identity that heartily welcomes, embraces and transcends our individuality and belongs to all those who have chosen to live with Unconditional Love in the Oneness.

We have written this book driven by the wish to share our healing journey, a trip through the illusions of the ego to our rebirth in the Oneness.

We have transmuted our experiences into Awareness and Love with the help of powerful, channeled energies that have, increasingly, guided and enlightened the path of our journey.

How many times have you heard someone say "We are all One"?

Has this resonated within you, as the greatest truth, each time you have heard it?

How difficult and painful is overcoming the ego?

How difficult is it to bring this truth from an ideal into our lives and our relationships?

This is what we have chosen to do, and this is what we have done.
This is our testimony.

With Love,
Human Angels

You can meet us on our web site www.wearehumanangels.com, on our Facebook page "We Are Human Angels" and on Twitter @HUMAN_ANGELS.

Table of contents

p. *07* *Foreword*

Introduction
p. 15 Are you a Human Angel?

Part 1
The 7 keys to overcome the ego
p. 21 The Oneness and the ego
  How to overcome the ego with the
  knowledge of the Oneness
p. 24 Judgment
  How to overcome the matrix of the
  ego
p. 27 Feelings of guilt
  How to stop self-destructive
  feelings
p. 30 Projections
  How to heal our romantic
  relationships
p. 34 Forgiveness
  How to free ourselves from the
  suffering of the past
p. 37 Fear
  How to overcome the illusion of
  fear
p. 40 Acceptance
  How to make the final transition
  from the ego to the Oneness

Part 2
The 7 keys to live with the heart in service to the Oneness

p. 47   The Rebirth
           How to be a Human Angel
p. 50   The Intelligence of the Heart
           How to consciously create our own reality
p. 53   Integrity
           How to be yourself without judgment
p. 56   The Here and Now
           How to live free from the past and the future
p. 59   Free Will
           How to help others while respecting their choices
p. 62   Silence
           How a Human Angels prays
p. 65   The Greater Good
           How to live in service to the Oneness

Appendix
p. 71   Being Human Angels
p. 73   About the Authors

OTHER BOOKS
BY HUMAN ANGELS

365 Wisdom Pills
Your daily dose of Angelic Wisdom

Our beloved Angels have inspired us to write this book that contains 365 simple, yet profound, Pills of Wisdom.

These Pills of Wisdom will give you faith, support and instant help for your spiritual growth.

The journey towards the Consciousness that we are all One is sometimes difficult with pitfalls created by our egos to keep us glued to our old beliefs.

During this journey, you might sometimes feel lost and lonely, searching for help and inspiration. In this case, *"365 Wisdom Pills"* is the remedy that, providing you with a daily dose of angelic wisdom, will strengthen you and jump-start your healing process.

"365 Wisdom Pills" will give you a new, enlightened perspective on your entire life.

"365 Wisdom Pills" is the first medicine that contains the active substance called "Soul Consciousness" and has only positive

and long-lasting effects on your spiritual health and self-worth.

The *Wisdom Pills* are recommended to start the healing process, from small to large emotional wounds and to reawaken the highest potential of every human being: their Divine Nature, the inner Human Angel that is waiting to be activated by the bright light of Consciousness. The *Wisdom Pills* act directly on those parts of yourself that need to be brought into balance.

Wisdom Pills will help you to remember the wonderful, Divine being that is You.

"365 Wisdom Pills" is available on all major on line bookstores. All information about the book and the stores can be found on our site:

www.wearehumanangels.com/365-wisdom-pills/.

365 Mantras for Today
Heal your life
Awaken the Human Angel within yourself
Awaken the Divine you

"365 Mantras for today" is a collection of original sentences written by ourselves and have been previously posted on our famous Facebook page *"We are Human Angels"*. These Mantras have already helped many people in finding their own path, bringing them light and inspiration and so now the authors have chosen to collect all of these mantras in a book wishing that, day by day, they will lovingly guide you in your everyday life journey.

These Mantras are based on synchronicity: in fact, there is not a calendar that assigns to each day a specific sentence. It is up to you to choose your daily mantra, simply guided by your Divine Self and by the energies that come into your life in the Here and Now.

Each mantra that you make your own, will become a ray of light that you turn on within yourself until you, free from every darkness and every fear, become a shining beacon that spreads its light into the world.

The book is available on all major on line bookstores, as an ebook and in paperback. Also available in Portuguese under the title *"365 Mantras para Hoje"*.
All information can be found here:

www.wearehumanangels.com/365-mantras-for-today/.

Made in the USA
San Bernardino, CA
07 January 2014